THIS NOTEBOOK BELONGS TO:

www.ingramcontent.com/pod-product-compliance
Lightning Source LLC
Chambersburg PA
CBHW021849170526
45157CB00007B/3007
9781090502636